LIAR

The Art of Detecting Deception
and
Eliciting Responses

By

Barry McManus

Global Traveler LLC
Leesburg, VA 20176
www.liarbook.com

ISBN: 978-0-9815855-0-5
Library of Congress Control Number: 2008924652

Cover Design by HighLevelStudios.com
Jacket Photograph by Susan Mezzulo
Book layout and design by Just Ink courtesy of High Level
Studios
www.highlevelstudios.com

This book is printed on acid-free paper

This book is dedicated to First Lieutenant Kurt Martine
28th MP CO Pennsylvania National Guard

"For a long time I have not said what I believe nor do I ever believe what I say and if indeed I do happen to tell the truth, I hide it among so many lies that it is hard to find."

Niccole Machiavelli

PREFACE

This book is a definitive resource for any information collector, whether a government collector, a law enforcement investigator, or a competitive intelligence collector in the private sector.

"Freedom is a privilege the people of the United States have chosen to embrace and have fought to protect throughout its history. It is the moral fiber that allows peoples from varying cultures to live together in peace and prosperity. To maintain this freedom and keep its spirit strong, we must learn to understand and appreciate the differences among cultures in our society. It is this understanding that will enable our law enforcement and intelligence communities to determine who among us is a friend or possible foe."

The material you are about to read has its genesis in the aftermath of the 9/11 attacks on New York City and Washington, D.C. Let us take a brief look at the activities leading up to this terrible tragedy.

Twenty-six al-Qaeda terrorist conspirators – eighteen Saudis, two Emiratis, one Egyptian, one Lebanese, one Moroccan, one Pakistani, and two Yemenis – sought to enter the United States for the specific purpose of carrying out a suicide mission. The first members of this team began to acquire the means to enter the United States two years and five months before the 9/11 attacks.

Intelligence authorities knew or suspected three of these conspirators to be al-Qaeda operatives (terrorists) in early 2000. However, their biographic information was not fully developed or provided to American Embassies abroad or posted at points of entry into the United States.

Three of the conspirators carried Saudi Arabian passports that contained possible extremist indicators. This indicator had been found in the passports of many al-Qaeda terrorists entering the United States as early as the first World Trade Center attack in 1993. This indicator had not been fully analyzed by the CIA, the FBI or our border authorities for its significance. Two of the conspirators carried passports containing fraudulent entry/exit stamps (or cachets) probably inserted into the passport by al-Qaeda travel document forgers.

In April 1999, the conspirators began to acquire entry visas to the United States. Two of the conspirators lied on their visa applications in detectable ways but were never questioned about these lies. Two other conspirators were interviewed for reasons unrelated to terrorism but most of the conspirators simply had their applications approved and their passports stamped with a United States visa without anything more than cursory examination of their documents. At that time, State Department Consular officials were not trained to detect potential terrorists they might encounter during a visa interview.

Once the operation was under way, the conspirators attempted to enter the United States 34 times over 21 months, through nine different airports. They succeeded all but once! Border Inspectors at United States airports were unaware of the potential significance of indicators of possible terrorist affiliation in the conspirators' passports and had no information about the fraudulent travel stamps possibly associated with al-Qaeda.

No Inspectors or Special Agents were trained in terrorist travel patterns or fraudulent document practices. Few of these Inspectors or Special Agents had interviewing skills acquired in any fashion beyond on-the-job training. More importantly, the culture these inspectors worked in focused on timely facilitation of a traveler's entry into the United States as opposed to enforcing Immigration rules and regulations. Noted exceptions to this practice included people suspected of carrying drugs or known criminals suspected of carrying contraband.

Five of the conspirators attempting entry were referred to secondary inspections for more intensive security screening. One pilot was referred to secondary inspection at two ports of entry, in one case by Customs Inspectors trained to look for drug couriers, and in the other by an Immigration Inspector thinking the pilot might be an intended immigrant. One pilot was referred to secondary inspection for having the wrong visa, and one non-pilot hijacker for failing to have a visa. Two other conspirators were referred to secondary inspection for failing to complete their arrival and customs forms and for being unable to communicate with the inspectors.

Four conspirators were admitted after the secondary inspectors who interviewed them did not, or were unable to, verify information supplied to them by the operative. In addition, misunderstandings of the Immigration laws, rules and regulations resulted in conspirators being allowed entry in the United States.

One conspirator was interviewed at length by a border inspector. The inspector concluded, on the basis of the conspirator's hostile and arrogant behavior and contradictory statements, that he was unlikely to comply with US Immigration law and posed a risk. He was denied entry but only after the inspector's decision was backed up by a supervising officer who acted in the face of a general expectation of leniency towards Saudi citizens at that airport.

These entries occurred during a period when approximately 20 million people applied for US entry visas, and more than 10 million people came into the United States through 220 ports of entry. During this period the 19 hijackers immersed themselves into American culture. They acquired driver's licenses, identification cards, places to live, work and study. They evaded the scrutiny of local and state police during routine traffic stops. In short, they became our next-door neighbors as well as the terrorists among us!

9/11 Commission
9/11 Terrorist Travel Report

CONTENTS

Chapter one discusses the technological advances in the detection of deception that have been monumental over the past few years. Ultimately, scientists may discover an infallible way of technologically determining whether or not a person is being truthful or deceptive about an issue in question. However, even when given an infallible scientific technique to use, the best a scientific instrument is ever going to provide you is a definitive statement of fact or probability as to whether or not the suspect in question is being truthful or practicing deception. With this information in hand, you will still have to employ elicitation skills to develop information the suspect is alleged to be hiding. It is important for you to employ elicitation skills to maintain a heightened awareness of elicitation methods currently employed by today's law enforcement and intelligence professionals.

There are no absolute, infallible ways to detect deception based solely on behavioral analysis. Chapter two will address how you can become a better collector of information using behavioral analysis as a complement to your elicitation skills.

Chapter three will empower you with winning interview strategies designed to help you carry out a successful information gathering event. It is necessary to plan ahead what you are aiming to resolve or determine from the interview process.

Rapport is a must for conducting a successful interview as information will flow from the relationship rapport established between the interviewer and the Subject. In Chapter four, you will learn various methods proven successful to establish rapport with individuals regardless of their background.

There are no fool-proof recipes for detecting deception and eliciting information; however, information is the best defense, as well as the most viable weapon in resolving any conflict, terrorism being no exception. The journey we are about to take in Chapter five is designed to give law enforcement, intelligence officers, and other in need of collecting credible and reliable information, the tools necessary to improve their ability to gather valid and factual information.

The primary goal of the interview is to elicit truthful and relevant information, not to obtain an admission of guilt. You should strive to get the person talking and keep him or her talking by using the appropriate question(s). Chapter six illustrates question techniques and formats designed to help you better understand the art of the question, and keep you in control of the interview.

Chapter seven builds on previous chapters and helps move the interview forward. The purpose of providing a story is to suggest a justification or motive for a person's action which allows him or her to provide additional information without "losing face."

A countermeasure is any behavioral tactic designed to defeat the purpose of the interview. A person may use countermeasures during the interview, and the degree to which he attempts to defeat the interview may be a measure of his involvement in terrorist or criminal activities. In Chapter eight, you will learn to identify and overcome countermeasures.

The purpose of chapter nine is to promote cross-cultural understanding so that local, state and federal law enforcement officers can better understand the vast majority of people from around the world who are law abiding citizens and allow officers and agents to better target those who intend to harm us.

The ability to persuade others is not in itself abnormal. It is also not extraordinary to lie, misrepresent and to deceive. As far as special techniques for the identification and successful persuasion of victims, there is very little evidence in literature which suggests that deceivers have any special sensitivity or gifts of insights into the minds of others. The deceiver's confidence, freedom from remorse, lack of affection or empathy for others, the enjoyment of acting and theater and the use of hyperbole are all assets in operations. When a systematized approach is added to the skills of a deceiver, as for example, the understanding of the culture, beliefs and ideologies of a particular target, he becomes prey to skilled operatives.

As for the victim (the deceived), the literature provides us very few clues as to what influences the deceived to develop trust to what the deceiver is saying or what he or she is doing.

INTRODUCTION

Detecting Deception – The Tools of the Trade or . . .
The Search for a Better Mousetrap!

Today, investigators have a multitude of technologies designed to assist them in their quest for the truth. This has not always been the case despite the fact that throughout history, determining the truth of a matter in question could routinely mean the difference between life and death.

In 500 B.C., Indian priests would put a donkey in a dark room and put lampblack on its tail. A group of suspected criminals were then brought into the dark room, and told that when the guilty party pulled the donkey's tail, "he would speak and be heard throughout the temple. The person who pulled the tail and had clean hands was pronounced the thief and punished."[1]

In medieval England, trial by ordeal determined guilt or innocence. A suspected liar could be ordered to carry a red-hot iron bar, or walk across red-hot ploughshares. If the suspect was burned, that was proof he was lying and he would be executed.[2] Other courts employed trial by water, with the accused being put into a sack and thrown into a pond. If the accused sank, he was deemed to be innocent. If he floated, it was taken as proof he was lying and he would be hung.[3]

During the 19th century, phrenology – the "measurement of bumps on a person's skull" led investigators to believe they could determine truth or deception by looking at and measuring a person's physical symptoms.[4] As time passed, the scientific community began looking at the chemical makeup of the suspected criminal's brain in search for a truth serum.[5]

Scopolamine, sodium amytal and sodium pentothal were, at times, given to suspects in the hopes of rendering them incapable of lying. [6] While these drugs caused the suspect to lose control of their thought and speech processes, "normally an endless stream of drug-addled gibberish" resulted leaving the investigators even more confused than they may have initially been. [7]

Today, investigators are aided by technical devices like the polygraph, voice stress analysis, facial thermal imaging, and magnetic resonance imaging. When used as a complement to a trained investigator's elicitation skills, these devices can serve to effectively focus the investigator's elicitation efforts in areas of specific concern to the suspect, thus improving the investigator's opportunity of eliciting information pertinent to the issue in question.

"It just seems to simplistic to condemn all lying. In the murkier grayness of the real world, choices must be made."

Henry Hyde
Iran-Contra Scandal in 1987

The Art of Detecting Deception

There is no silver bullet to lie detection and eliciting information, and anyone who tries to tell you differently is … well… DECEIVING you. In fact, most of the information about detecting deception and eliciting information is generic: it can be found in myriad of books, magazine and seminars. What I have discovered with over three decades of conducting interviews and interrogations in over 130 countries, is that despite nationality, citizenship, ethnicity, religious beliefs or lack thereof, or our level of professional stature, most of us, lie in basically the same fashion.

The Art of Detecting Deception and Eliciting Responses works cross-culturally, from foreign to local investors, to employees, executives and competing negotiating teams, and anyone else from whom you need to gain accurate information.

The Art of Detecting Deception and Eliciting Responses and the techniques learned to elicit information and assess behavior will not make you a James Darrell or a Perry Mason, it will not turn your facility into a Fort Knox, and it will not alienate your company from potential clients or employees. Rather, it is a risk management tool that helps you assess the potential vulnerabilities to deception. It is designed not to limit you, but to increase your probability of success. Being confident that you and your team are acting on reliable, credible, and true information can only increase your ability to reach your company, institution, or organization's overall objectives.

Ask an interviewee, a suspect, or a witness a question, and you can begin to detect deception in as little as three to five seconds as you establish their baseline of behavior. But, the primary goal of an interview is to elicit information, not to determine guilt or innocence. The Art of Detecting Deception and Eliciting Responses is not meant to turn you and your associates into interrogators. In fact, the difference between interviewing and interrogation is vast.

The Art of Detecting Deception and Eliciting Responses is a structured behavioral analysis methodology for conducting more effective interviews. This methodology will enable you, your company, institution, and/or organization to recognize deceptive statements and behavior, and ultimately get the information you need. The recent corporate scandals of WorldCom, Enron, Anderson, Adelphi, Xerox, Tyco, Global Crossing, Qwest, and Merrill Lynch, and others, clearly demonstrate that today's businesses simply cannot afford the risks of unchecked deception – whether within the company's ranks, or in that of its partners and clients. Lost revenue, damaged public trust, and the levying of legal and financial penalties are just some of these risks. Today's executives must be able to quickly and effectively identify deceptive business tactics within their company and from outside parties. The Art of Detecting Deception and Eliciting Responses is specifically designed to aid those of us in the board room to those of us on the borders protecting our country; it applies to the issues of legal, financial, human resource, security, law enforcement, and crisis management.

Chapter 1 The Technology
The Polygraph

The modern polygraph employs attachments that monitor the pulmonary and cardiovascular activity and electrodermal responses that one's body undergoes when exposed to specific stressors. These "stressors" take the form of a variety of questions arrayed in a particular testing format. Current technology employs a digital converter linked to either a stand-alone or networked desktop or laptop computer to convert physiological "signals" monitored by the attachments into digital signals transmitted to a video display monitor that allows the examiner to visualize the person's physiology as it changes throughout the course of the test. By comparing physiological responses over the course of a number of comparative tests, an examiner can make a determination as to whether or not the person is being truthful or deceptive.

The technology has not always been this complex. In fact, the technology involved in deception detection evolved slowly over many years. In 1895, Cesare Lombroso first attempted to detect deception by employing scientific means. Lombroso's plethysmograph measured changes in the blood flow of a person undergoing interrogation.[8]

In 1897, B. Sticker measured the galvanic skin response of a person undergoing interrogation by monitoring the electrical conductivity of one's skin while sweating during interrogation.[9]

In 1914, Vittorio Benussi used pneumatic tubing to measure people's respiration rates. Benussi found that the "ratio of inspiration and expiration was generally greater before truth telling than that before lying,"[10]

Benussi's work with respiration rates meant that blood pressure; galvanic skin response and respiration rates could all be used to monitor a person's physiology when confronted with questions addressing a specific issue for the purpose of making a determination as to whether or not a person is being truthful or deceptive.

It was not until 1915 that William Marston, an American psychologist, began to demonstrate a "lie detection test" that used a blood pressure cuff to monitor the suspect's systolic blood pressure during interrogation.[11] Marston was not so much interested in the technology employed during the interrogation, but rather, believed it to be the <u>interrogation techniques</u> that the technology complemented that made the detection of deception possible.[12]

In 1921, John Larson created the first "polygraph" to be used by forensic scientists.[13] Larson's "cardio-pneumo-psychogram" monitored blood pressure, pulse and respiratory rates and recorded them on a drum of paper.[14] This was the first time anyone attempted to employ technology to simultaneously monitor several physiological responses for the purpose of detecting deception.

Leonard Keeler improved upon Larson's design by adding a "kymograph," a motor that turned at a regular rate of speed that served to rotate the drum of paper rolling underneath the pens.[15.]

He also improved upon the quality of the tubes used to measure his Subject's respiration rate and installed a "psycho-galvanometer"[16] that monitored galvanic skin response via two small metal plates that he attached to his Subject's fingertips.[17]

Keeler started to market the "Keeler Polygraph" in 1926, touting it as a "lie detector." Keeler succeeded in convincing the law enforcement community that his "lie detector" was just that, an infallible way of detecting deception.

Technology remained unchanged for nearly 20 years. In 1946, the Stoelting Company introduced electronic recording channels, making it the first company to have recording channels that enabled the examiner to electronically enhance the amplitude of the polygraph tracings by simply adjusting a sensitivity knob on the front plate of the instrument's face. It was on this type of polygraph instrument that I received my first technical polygraph training in 1982.

In 1968, Stoelting introduced its cardio activity monitor (CAM) and began to improve upon the versatility of its instruments by producing multi-function electronic components.[18] In the late 1980s, the first computer assisted polygraph was introduced to the marketplace and in 1992, and Stoelting introduced its "Computerized Polygraph System."[19]

Today, computer software algorithms allow Forensic Pyscho-physiologists to monitor a digital signal displayed on a laptop or desktop computer monitor. Forensic Pyscho-physiologists are also able to visually enhance the quality of the polygraph tracings. The improved signal tracing quality purportedly increases the likelihood of an accurate diagnostic analysis. Forensic Pyscho-physiologists can increase or decrease the amplitude of the component tracings, visually dampen the effects of an erratic cardio signal and eliminate cardio contamination caused by premature ventricular contractions. In addition, Forensic Pyschophysiologists can visually compare one chart against another on a split display screen, run scoring algorithms against relevant questions to determine the probability of deception and communicate with their manager via the computer's communication system while the test is in progress. Systems of this nature are currently in use in the majority of the polygraph programs throughout the law enforcement and intelligence community.

The use of the polygraph has always been controversial. The legal profession casts doubts on its evidentiary value, with most courts refusing to admit polygraph test results into evidence. The scientific community has questioned the technology employed in the polygraph process and is constantly looking to build a better mousetrap. Congress has joined the fray by passing the *Employee Polygraph Protection Act of 1988*, which limits the use of the polygraph as a pre-employment screening tool in the vast majority of industries. (See *The Employee Polygraph Protection Act of 1988*, P.L. 100-347, June 27, 1988). Despite this controversy, the use of polygraph testing for employment screening, and as an investigative tool, is still prevalent among law enforcement and intelligence agencies, as well as selected industries involved in high-risk activities (i.e. the pharmaceutical and nuclear industries), with tens of thousands of tests being conducted each year. In this writer's professional opinion, given a properly trained forensic psychophysiologist, properly calibrated instrumentation, and a specific issue on which to work, the polygraph is still the best tool available for the detection of deception and will continue to play an integral role in both the law enforcement and intelligence communities.

Voice Stress Analysis

Attempts at detecting deception through the analysis of the change in stress levels in one's voice have been ongoing since the early 1970s. Charles McQuiston developed the psychological stress evacuator (PSE) to assist American soldiers in Vietnam "interrogate prisoners of war without appearing to obviously test for lies."[20] Offspring of the PSE include the voice stress analyzer (VSA) and the computerized voice stress analyzer (CVSA).

In principle, voice stress analysis involves a simple technology that monitors the changing frequencies in one's vocal chords when subjected to moments of stress. Research has shown that "[a]all muscles in the body, including the vocal chords, vibrate in the 8 to 12 Hz range. . . . In moments of stress, like when you tell a lie that you dare not get caught at, . . . [t]heir vibration increases from the relaxed 8 to 9 Hz, to the stressful 11 to 12 Hz range."[21] The one commonality among all people is "that their stress levels are constantly changing within their current range, changes which indicate the 'perceived jeopardy' or 'danger' of statements being made."[22] As a lie often harbors severe consequences, the danger of incurring these consequences results in the person's stress level significantly increasing. The ensuing increase in the vocal stress level is relatively easy to monitor using the VSA or CVSA.

The Defense Academy for Credibility Assessment (DACA) formerly the Department of Defense Polygraph Institute (DoDPI) routinely conducts research for federal government programs involving the technology associated with detecting deception. One such study, "Ability of the Vericator™ to Detect Smugglers at a Mock Security Checkpoint" (February 2003) found reliability rates of the CVSA to be so low that they could not recommend use of the instrument for detecting deception at that time.[23] DoDPI went on to note:

Undoubtedly, the allure of VSA will continue into the foreseeable future for a number of reasons. First, the acquisition of vocal signals does not require sensors or transducers to come in contact with or be visible to the person being monitored. . . . Second, the acquisition of vocal signals does not require expensive and cumbersome equipment. . . . Third, the acquisition of vocal signals can be made during various formats, e.g. interrogations, interviews, and unstructured conversations. . . . [F]fourth . . . there is an established VSA industry that has been in operation for 30 years. . . . [F]fifth . . . VSA will continue . . . [to put] pressure on legislators and program managers to provide quick solutions to long-term problems. . . . [Finally] . . . is the intuitive belief that stress and deception can be determined by listening to a person speak? VSA, therefore, becomes a magical "silver bullet" in people's mind. Unfortunately, to date, VSA still has not proven to be a valid and reliable indicator of stress or deception.[24] Despite these findings, there are police agencies and private security firms that encourage the use of VSA (or the CVSA) as a complement to their investigative capabilities.

Emerging Technology

There are a number of emerging technologies currently available that may be applicable to the detection of deception. Facial thermal imaging allows users to map one's facial blood flow. "When a person lies, he . . . often becomes anxious and excessive blood flows to areas around the eyes. This blood flow can be detected by a thermal imaging screener."[25]

Lasers can now be used "to detect muscular, circulatory, and other bodily changes assumed to be associated with the anxiety of lying."[26] There is even a "lie-detecting keyboard,"[27] which the developer maintains can "detect lies when a person types into a computer by analyzing typing patterns, sensing moisture in fingertips, recording body heat, and monitoring how fast the fingers were moving when they hit the keyboard."[28]

Researchers have recently "discovered that certain regions of the brain exhibit unique activity during lying. . . ."[29] [T]he anterior cingulate cortex is one of these regions.[30] Increased neural activity "can be detected by functional magnetic resonance imaging (MRI), which records brain activity by identifying changes in brain blood flow and metabolic rate."[31]

Lawrence Farwell, a former Harvard Medical School faculty member, has developed what he has called "brain finger-printing."[32] This technique commences "before a person even has the chance to lie by looking for a telltale brainwave after a Subject is flashed a cue having something to do with the crime. . . . This brainwave only appears if the person has a memory of that information stored in their brain."[33] Farwell believes that this technique may have application in the war against terrorism. "If someone has undergone training as a terrorist, they have that information stored in their brain and we can detect it."[34] Whether or not this technique has practical application remains to be seen.

As you can see, the technological advances in the detection of deception have been monumental over the past few years. Ultimately, scientists may discover an infallible way of tech-nologically determining whether or not a person is being truthful or deceptive about an issue in question. However, even given an infallible scientific technique, the best a scientific instrument is ever going to be able to give an investigator is a definitive statement of fact or probability as to whether or not the suspect in question is being truthful or practicing deception. With this information in hand, the investigator will still have to employ his elicitation skills to develop the information the suspect is alleged to be hiding resulting in the need for a heightened awareness of the importance of the elicitation methods currently employed by today's law enforcement and intelligence professionals.

Chapter 2 Detecting Deception
Signs of Deception

There are no absolute, infallible ways to detect deception based solely on behavioral analysis. However, when used as a complement to your elicitation skills, you can become a better collector of information. You must understand that one person can be both truthful and deceptive when conveying a story, as every good story must have an element of truth to it in order to be believable.

You must understand that you should never conduct an interview looking for truthful behavior. Why?

Focusing your efforts on trying to identify truthful behavior, may result in your missing or misinterpreting deceptive behavior.

Truthful behavior can be learned! This action, which we refer to as countermeasures, may result in truthful behavior being mimicked by a person practicing deception. We'll discuss countermeasures in depth in Chapter 10.

Signs of Truthful Behavior

The following indicators are generally indicative of truthful behavior, cross-culturally, and can serve as a behavioral baseline for your initial assessment. For example:

Direct "yes" or "no" responses.
   Interviewer: Is your name John Doe (if this has been verified)?
   Subject: Yes.
   Interviewer: Has anyone asked you to carry anything for them today?
   Subject: No.

Answering questions with specificity (not overly specific):
   Interviewer: Who are you meeting with?
   Subject: I am meeting with my brother, John. He lives here.

Verbal and non-verbal responses are compatible:
   Interviewer: Have you been to the United States before?
   Subject: Uh, no, (Shakes head affirmatively while answering negatively.)

Responses are spontaneous, with little or no hesitation (be careful of complex questions):
   Interviewer: Where are you staying while you are here?
   Subject: With my cousin.
   Interviewer: Where are you staying? How are you getting there?
   Subject: (pause) I am taking a taxi.

Attentive, composed, and interested:
   Interviewer: I need to ask you some additional questions.
   Subject: No problem. Have I done something wrong? (Subject looks directly at Interviewer.)

Appropriate body posture

Subject: Open – arms not crossed or covering the body. Sitting up straight or leaning in towards interviewer.

Examples:

- "Sincere" smile
- Appropriate eye contact (does not stare)
- Sits erect and does not slouch lean away from Interviewer

Signs of Deceptive Behavior

Look for deceptive behavior with an eye to:

Critical Timeframes

- Behaviors demonstrated during the Critical Timeframe From "Point of Question Stimulation" (PQS) to "Point of Question Recognition" (PQR) to 3 to 5 seconds beyond "Point of Question Answer" (PQA).

Example:

Were you born in Baghdad?   Yes

>   >   >
PQS   PQR   PQA
                         [<3 -5 Seconds >]
              [< Critical Timeframe   >]

Combinations/Clusters

- 2 or more deceptive behaviors occurring within that Critical Timeframe

Examples of Deceptive Behaviors:

Repeats your questions

Interviewer: Is this your first time in the United States?

Subject: "Is this my first time in the United States?

Provides overly specific explanations:

Interviewer: Who will be picking you up?

Subject: Well Officer, James is my mother's sister son, and he should be like a brother to me but instead he is very distant did not even offer to pick me up form the train station after all we have done for him.

Provides a non-answer:

Subject: "That's a good question."

Too happy, or too friendly / overly polite (thankful and overly complimentary):

Subject: I understand officer you are just doing your job.

Tendency to qualify answers:

Subject: Honestly, I didn't do it.

Invokes religion:

Subject: I would never do anything like that; I am a good (person, Christian, Muslim etc.)

Fails to understand a simple question:

Interviewer: Are you traveling alone?

Subject: What do you mean by traveling alone?

Selective memory

Subject: I don't recall; I just can't remember.

Officer: Where do they live?

Subject: In Washington, DC.

Officer: What is their address?

Subject: Ah, I don't have that information with me it's in my suitcase.

Officer: How do you plan to meet your parents?

Subject: I was going to call them once I arrived.

Officer: If we called them, would they confirm that you are coming to visit?

Subject: No, ah, I was going to surprise them.

Officer: How were you going to get to Washington, DC?

Subject: I was going to take a cab.

Were you able to identify several of Ms. Malik's deceptive behaviors that registered with the questions?

Select the signs of deception you observed. (Select all that apply.):

1. Response 1: Provides a non-answer.
2. Response 2: Provides a protest.
3. Response 3: Repeats your questions
4. Response 4: Tendency to qualify answers.
5. Response 5: Gross shifts, body movements
6. Response 6: Backward movement.
7. Response 7: Grooming gestures.
8. Response 8: Inappropriate posture.

Analysis

Did you notice her gross body shifts and movements when

she responded *"Ah, I am not certain, maybe three weeks"*. Her signs of discomfort when she was questioned on her mode of transportation to her parents and she responded *"I was going to call them once I arrived."* (Almost, asking the officer the question and not the answer.) Ms. Malik even decided to use an objection when she was to provide the names of her parents and she responded *"Why is that important officer?"* instead of answering the officer's question.

The Interviewee did not repeat Officers Jones questions, nor provided non-answers. This Interviewee did not have the tendency to qualify answers or use behavioral pauses or inappropriate eye movement.

Correct responses

Correct answers: 1, 2, 5, and 8

Now let's try another one. List the signs of deception.

B. Sarin Gas Attack

Officer: My name is Officer Jones. How would you like me to address you?

Subject: You may call me Ali.

Officer: Ali, we are investigating the attempted Sarin attack on a local cruise ship. What knowledge do you have of this event?

Subject: I have heard of this ship but have no knowledge of the events you describe.

Officer: Ali, what was your involvement in this cruise ship attack?

Subject: Officer. Why would you say I was involved?

Officer: Why would someone say they overheard you talking about an attack on a cruise ship?

Subject: They were mistaken.

Officer: Ali, I don't believe you are telling me the truth.

Subject: Why do you ask me these types of questions? I am in your custody; I can do you no harm.

Great! Were you able to identify several of Ali's deceptive behaviors that registered with the questions? Select the signs of deception you observed. (Select all that apply.)

1. Response 1: Provides a non-answer.
2. Response 2: Provides a protest.
3. Response 3: Repeats your questions

4. Response 4: Tendency to qualify answers.
5. Response 5: Provides a non-verbal response

Analysis

Did you observe Ali's non-answer when he responded to the officer's question?

Officer: Ali, what was your involvement in the cruise ship attack?

Ali: Officer, Why would you say I was involved?

Ali, utilized a protest when confronted by Officer Jones, telling him, "Ali, I don't believe you are telling me the truth."

Ali: "Why do you ask me these types of questions? I am in your custody; I can do you no harm."

If you selected any of the other signs of deception you may need to re-calibrate or establish a second behavioral pattern of Ali. Although all the other selections are deceptive responses, Ali did not repeat Officer Jones questions, qualify his answers or provide any non-verbal responses.

Correct responses:
Correct answers: 1 and 2

C. Murder Suspect

Here we have the requirement to interview a suspected assailant responsible for the brutal murders of four members of an Arab-American family. The victims, Coptic Christians from Egypt, died of multiple stab wounds. The focus of the interview is to determine Subject's involvement and the motive of the crime.

See how many signs of deception you identified correctly.

Officer: My name is Officer Jones. How would you like me to address you?

Subject: You may call me Ayman

Officer: Ayman, what happened last night? Was it just a misunderstanding or did you just get upset and lose your temper?

Subject: Right at this moment I am just confused. You are not telling me anything.

Officer: Are you confused about the incident or the reasons that prompted the killings.

Subject: (Silence)

Select the signs of deception. (Select all that apply.)
1.   Response 1: Non-answer
2.   Response 2: failure to answer a simple question.
3.   Response 3: Selective memory.
4.   Response 4: Overly specific explanation.
5.   Response 5: Behavioral pause.

Analysis

The Subject demonstrated deceptive behaviors when he responded to the officer's questions. These deceptive behaviors included his non-answer and behavioral pause.

Correct responses:
Correct answers: 1 and 5

D. A Terrorist Look-out

A traveler is applying for admission into the United States. He is referred to a secondary interview after a US Customs and Border Protection Officer discovers that Subject is a possible match to a person on the current terrorist watch list. It was determined during further checks that the Subject is not that person. However, the interview continues.

As you read the following questions and answers, list the signs of deception. How many signs of deception did you identify correctly?

Officer: Hello, may I see your passport, ticket and declaration card. Where are you coming from today?
Subject: Morocco transiting London
Officer: Where are traveling to?
Subject: New York.
Officer: What is the purpose of your visit?
Subject: To attend a conference in New York.
Officer: Is this your first time in this country?
Subject: Ah, yes.
Officer: Where will you be staying?
Subject: In a hotel.
Officer: What is the name and address of the hotel in which you are staying?
Subject: Ah, I don't have that information with me.
Officer: Tell me, what do you do in Morocco?
Subject: Why is that important for you to know?
Officer: It's simply part of the pre-entry interview Sir.
Subject: Ah, okay, well, I do scientific work.
Officer: What type of science?

Subject: Nuclear science.
Officer: What is the conference about?
Subject: Nuclear science.

1. Response 1: Provides a non-answer.
2. Response 2: Stutters.
3. Response 3: Complains.
4. Response 4: Not specific enough.
5. Response 5: Behavioral pauses, delay

Analysis

Okay! Were you able to identify several of the Interviewee's deceptive behaviors that registered with the questions asked? His non-answer, when Officer Jones asks the Subject, "Tell me, what you do in Morocco?" and responded, "Why is that important for you to know?" The Subject also demonstrated another deceptive clue when he provided a non-specific response to Officer Jones.

Correct responses:
Correct answers: 1 and 4

Helpful tip: Occasionally, Interviewers may need to recalibrate or establish a second behavioral pattern of the Subject to identify deceptive behaviors or other indicators not previously displayed, such as, stuttering, complaints, eye blinks, grooming gestures or behavioral pauses and delays.

Summary: Deception Detection

In the end, the most important thing to remember is to closely note behaviors occurring within the critical timeframe and that which occurs in combinations and/or clusters.

Look for deceptive behavior indicators with an eye to the following considerations:

Timing

- Behaviors demonstrated during the timeframe (From "Point of Question Stimulation to the Point of Question

Recognition to the 3 to 5 seconds beyond "Point of Question Answer"

Combinations and Clusters

- 2 or more deceptive behaviors occurring within the critical timeframe

Chapter 3 Developing Interviewing Strategies
Interview Strategy

The purpose of the interview is to get your Subject, witness, victim, or source, talking and to keep them talking to gather accurate and reliable information, and not necessarily to obtain admissions of guilt or wrongdoing. How do you convince someone to provide information that is not in his/her best interest? Preparation is understanding who you are interviewing. This requires preparation and when preparation is not possible, depending on your field, you can prepare by reading and studying about people and their culture. When possible, read whatever information is at your disposal, talk to those with knowledge of the Subject, their culture, or geographical knowledge. Additionally, develop a strategy, a game plan. With time, as you develop expertise, you will have a list (suitcase, shopping list) of various strategies that have worked depending on different interview scenarios. This does not mean that these strategies will work always for everyone. It means you must have a game plan and be flexible enough to switch gears as needed if your strategies are not working.

Good preparation increases your ability to establish rapport. Why?

If you have done your homework in understanding the person's culture, identifying possible areas of commonality and potential problem areas, this will lead you to a strategy that will include question formulation and theme and story development.

Interview Strategies

The greatest mistake made by interviewers is the absence of preparation before the interview begins. Let's take a look of some of those key issues in gathering data points before the interview:

- Determine key issues and questions.

In order to carry out a successful information gathering exercise, it is necessary to plan ahead what you are aiming to resolve or determine from the process. Have a strategy outlined as early as possible and make sure you cover all areas that you previously planned out during the information gathering stage. Use systemic queries on the Subject if you do not receive the depth of detail in answers to questions that you are posing.

- Consider options for questions.

Review your questioning techniques and interviewing strategy before the information gathering phase. Make sure that you adapt your line and method of questioning to meet circumstances. If the Subject you are speaking to is non-communicative, work on building more of a rapport with them. If the Subject is overly verbose in their response, if they seem to be redirecting the questions you are asking and answering something else, do not hesitate to steer the discussion back on topic.

- Incorporate soft language.

In all instances, be low key – your goal is to gather information, not intimidate the Subject. Do not damage rapport;

it is very difficult to build a successful rapport with a Subject and very, very easy to lose it over a misspoken phrase or a shift in attitude that creates a raft between you and the Subject.

- Consider the timing and priority. Ask the least anxious and threatening questions first.

Be systematic. Think of the information gathering effort as a game of egos. Each question you pose is another counter on the board. Select your question/moves carefully and at all times keep the larger picture in mind. There is no silver bullet to getting the answers you want, but if you systematically approach the issue from a variety of angles and approaches you are more likely to get more of the information that you want. At the same time, as in any game of egos, watch your opponents' moves as well and make sure that you're not being bracketed into a topic that deviates too far from your goal. You get to make the first move and set some of the rules on the board so make sure to carefully plan and implement your strategy.

Conducting the Interview

It would be nice if we could identify a photo of the ideal interview room (a nice quiet place…)

A cornerstone of an interview that will yield the most reliable information is an effective, ongoing assessment of the Subject and the environment and the around them. In evaluating these factors the following are keys.

- Privacy is important.
Privacy is a key opponent to the success of any interview.

- Initially, keep note-taking to a minimum until rapport is established.
- Be prepared to take notes.
- Assess the behavior.

As it is important that you assess the Subject's behavior, it is also as important that you avoid providing any information to the Subject by shifting your body position, looking overly interested on any one particular issue, or writing more notes when valuable information is being provided. Remember, the job is to elicit information. Make certain that you record the Subject's appearance and behavioral mannerism, clothing, jewelry, etc.

The Interview Summary

The purpose of the interview is to gather accurate and reliable information that will further the security and safety of our nation and the people we serve. How do you convince someone to provide information that is not in his/her best interest? It's always important to employ a strategic approach to information elicitation. You should familiarize yourself with the question types you have at your disposal and know when and why you should use them.

Remember, the importance of effective questioning when eliciting information.

You may have to ask the same question in a number of different ways and forms to ensure you understand the Subject's answer. You need to know when to, how, and why to repeat questions to properly orchestrate the interview.

Ask the:
    Who?
    What?
    When?
    Where?
    Why?

In summary, the process of asking questions and knowing why we ask questions is paramount. Understanding who, what, when, where, and why are important parts of gathering reliable and accurate information. Sometimes asking detailed questions about every element may seem tedious but is necessary. You may find yourself asking 10 questions to finally get the necessary response from the subject although one or two should have sufficed.

Chapter 4 Rapport

Establishing rapport is a must for conducting a successful interview as information will flow from the relationship rapport establishes between the interviewer and his Subject.

Establishing rapport may not guarantee the Subject's cooperating with you in providing information, but failing to establish rapport will certainly impede your elicitation efforts.

Rapport is established the moment eye contact is first made and is continually built upon as personal interaction progresses.

Rapport is established by showing patience, sincerity and compassion for the people you're interviewing.

Failure to demonstrate any of these attributes shows insincerity or a lack of self-control.

Rapport can easily be developed and exploited if you make the effort to do so. Where it is possible, it helps to begin building rapport by first sharing experiences. "Did you have a good trip coming over? It may put him at ease and begin building a common ground between you. Once established, rapport can easily be lost. Let's look at some of the ways rapport can be lost.

- Lack of professionalism, including sloppy appearance.
- Casual approach and stance, such as leaning against a wall with hands in pockets or slouching.

- Downgrading status or profession – theirs or yours.
- Arrogant, officious, or judgmental behavior.
- Interrupting or finishing sentences. The Interviewer should instead be an active listener.
- Abruptly changing the Subject. The Interviewer should instead use transitions to introduce the next topic.
- Directly addressing a Middle Eastern man about his spouse or daughters.
- And, going for the "jugular." Subtlety is the key to your success in establishing rapport.

Making the Initial Contact

In making initial contact with a source, introduce yourself and ask a simple question or make a simple statement to confirm the Subject's name(s) suspect or witness, there are preliminary questions an Interviewer should prepare to ask that could enhance their introduction to the Subject, such as:

- How was your trip today?
- How was your flight?
- Is there anything I can do to make you more comfortable?

Following the introduction, ask a simple question or make a simple statement to confirm the Subject's name(s), such as:

- Please confirm your full legal name.
- What other names have you used?
- Can you write that out for me?

Confirm the person's full legal name and preferred way to be addressed. Also, ask them what other names they have used. If appropriate, have the individual write out his or her name. Having the correct spelling is very important. Do not leave it to chance.

Use the information provided to ask follow-up questions.

Listen and use the information provided in the responses to ask follow-up questions. You are now preparing to enter the elicitation phase of your questioning.

Look for commonalities, but be careful about supplying too much personal information about yourself and or your family.

Always keep the elements of information you are trying to obtain in the back of your mind.

- "Oh, I also have two sons…"
- "I grew up in the mid-west also."

An Officer/Agent brings a South Eastern Asian Subject into an interview room and leaves without saying a word. The officer/agent returns after having been gone for an extended period of time.

The Subject, a Pakistani male, appears startled and almost frightened, and his voice cracks in fear.

What Are Your Questions To Elicit Information From This Interviewee?

Using the scenario above, read the questions below, and select the question you think is correct.

Question 1 – Ok, what's your name, how old are you, and what's your date and place of birth. Oh, by the way where do you live?

Question 2 – Good morning Mr. Muhammad, I am Officer/ Agent Jones; I have a few questions I need to ask you as part of this investigation?

Question 3 – You look nervous? Why do you look so nervous?

Question 4 – Before you sit down please empty your pockets and let me see some form of identification.

If you selected Question 2, you are correct.

Helpful tip: If you have a nervous Subject, you should make efforts to calm the person and explain why they are being stopped before rushing into your questions.

Now, let's examine a few examples of how rapport can be damaged.

Scenario 1: Damaging Rapport

In this scenario, an Interviewer brings a Subject into an interview room and leaves her there without saying a word for a long time. Fifteen minutes later the officer returns.

Read on and identify what the Interviewer does to lose rapport.

The Interviewer shows little emotion and appears almost stoic. The Interviewer asks rapid fire questions.

Officer: Ok folks, let's get started here, what is your name, age, date and place of birth, and your address?

The Subject appears upset and disgusted but answers the questions.

Subject: My name is Samira, I am 34 years old. I am Egyptian by birth but I live here in the United States. I am a Legal Resident Alien. Please tell me why you have stopped me and why you are being so rude.

What went wrong?

What do you think went wrong here? Was the Subject too defensive? Was the officer too official?

Read below and see what Samira has to say about the interview.

Subject: Well, in my culture, you would never be as rude as this officer. Although, it appears that he is just doing his job, I was offended by his demeanor, his not telling me why he had stopped me, his abrupt manners and rapid style of questioning. It would have been better if he had recognized my nervousness and tried to calm me down by first starting a conversation designed to establish rapport before rushing right into his questions.

Re-establishing Rapport

Now, that you have learned what the officer did to offend Samira, let's see if he can start again with an effort to establish rapport.

This time the officer is sitting upright and looking attentive at Samira. The officer shows emotion by displaying sincere concern.

Officer: I am Officer Jones I have a few questions I need to ask you as part of our inspection process. Before we get started, is there something I can get for you to make you more comfortable?"

Subject: No, thank you.

Officer: I need to check some records but I will return in a few minutes. (Officer returns) Sorry for the delay, now let's get started. I need your full name, your date and place of birth and your current address for our records. We are sorry to inconvenience you but this is part of the routine inspection process.

Scenario 2: Damaging Rapport

In this scenario, an officer is interviewing a Middle Eastern man who is entering a US Port of Entry. Again, read how the officer handled the interview and identify what the Interviewer does to lose rapport.

The officer appears very impatient. The Interviewer shows his impatience by asking rapid-fire questions and constantly looking at his watch. The officer asks Subject, a Middle Eastern man, the following questions.

Officer: Where are you coming from today and where are you traveling to and are these all your bags?

The Subject appearing frustrated and annoyed frowns and remains silent.

What went wrong?

What do you think went wrong here? Was Officer Jones too quick in the beginning by asking his questions before establishing rapport? Should the officer have recognized that

Subject was uncomfortable with his rapid fire style of questioning? Read Subject's comments below regarding Officer Jones treatment.

Re-establishing Rapport:

In my culture, you would not want to begin asking questions as quickly and as abruptly as Officer Jones. It would be perceived as being rude. It would have been better if the officer had established some type of rapport.

Now, you have read what the officer did to offend Subject, let's see if he can start again with an effort towards establishing rapport.

This time Officer Jones is friendly and takes time to put Subject at ease before launching into questions.

Officer: Hello. My name is Officer Jones. May I see your passport, your ticket and your declaration card?
Subject: Yes.
Officer: The reason I stopped you today is part of the routine inspection process. Where are you coming from today?
Subject: Egypt.
Officer: And, where are you traveling to?
Subject: Washington, DC
Officer: Are these all your bags?
Subject: Yes.

Scenario 3: Damaging Rapport

In this scenario, an Interviewer approaches a Middle Eastern man and what appear to be members of his family. Now, let's read the scenario and identify what the Interviewer does here to lose rapport.

In this scenario, the Interviewer (a police officer) approaches Subject (a Middle Eastern man) and several Middle Eastern women.

Showing little emotion or caring, the police officer approaches Subject and asks the following:

Officer: Is that your mother?
Subject: (In apparent disbelief and appearing agitated) yes.
Officer: Do you have any sisters or brothers?
Subject: Yes.
Officer: Are these your sisters?
Subject: (Raising his voice, with a frown on his face) Why is that important to you? Why would you ask such personal questions?

What went wrong?

What went wrong here in this scenario? Were the Officer's questions too personal? Did he make a cultural faux pas? Read what the Subject has to say about the interview.

Re-establishing Rapport:

The Subject was offended by the probing questions about his family. It showed in his verbal and non-verbal behavior. In my culture, one's family is to be protected particularly one's female family members at all cost. Without specifically telling me why the officer needed information on members of my family, I would be reluctant to answer his questions. In the future, Officer Jones should be aware he's dealing with another culture and understand that in the Middle Eastern culture, and specifically the Muslim culture, for most part, he will get some resistance when questions are asked of our families without an appropriate explanation.

If you know the Subject is traveling with someone, but has not specifically mentioned that person, you may not want to ask direct closed-ended questions initially.

Can Officer Jones redeem himself? Let's read to find out.

This time Officer Jones is friendly which puts Subject more at ease. Officer Jones asks an open-ended question.

Officer: Tell me about your family?

Subject: Yes, I am married and I have two sons and two daughters.

Officer: Are you traveling with family members today?

Subject: Yes, my wife and sister.

Officer: Are there any other family members traveling with you today?

Subject: Yes, my mother-in-law.

Scenario 4: Damaging Rapport

Officer Jones is intense and is trained in interrogation techniques. He is trained to confront when he believes someone is lying, but is not necessarily conversed in the art of information collection. These techniques involve using the Subject's emotions, values, and self-perceptions to gain key information.

The next scenarios provide additional examples of situations where Officer Jones lost rapport with a Subject followed by the Subject's input on why the rapport was damaged and what could have been done to establish and maintain rapport to collect information.

Officer Jones directly confronts Subject, a Middle Eastern man.

Officer: You know what I don't believe you are here on vacation. Can you explain why you have the calendar, maps and flight information in your suitcase?"

Subject: Obviously emotional, his voice shakes as he responds, "I told you I am here to visit my brother. The calendar I will use to plan my trip to see the sights I have marked on the map."

The exchange becomes more heated as Officer Jones continues his confrontation.

Officer: Well, you don't know your brother's address or telephone number. I think you're lying to me!"

Subject: I'm not lying to you. Why would you say something like that to me?

Officer: Please tell us the truth (Officer Jones moves in closer to Subject and touches his arm). We have seen many cases like yours, where young innocent people like you are asked to do bad things for bad people.

What went wrong?

Was Officer Jones too officious in his duties? Did he establish rapport with Subject? Did he consider cultural sensitivities? What about his touching Subject? Was that appropriate? Let's get insight from Subject.

In my culture, direct confrontation is not always best. Typically, aggressive behavior, confrontation and threats are not well accepted by people from the Middle East. As an educated man, it would have been better if the officer showed some genuine interest in me and the mistakes I might have made.

Re-establishing Rapport

Now that we have more insight into the cultural sensitivities and ways to establish rapport, let's see how Officer Jones handles the situation this time.

In a lower, slower, and even-keeled tone of voice, Officer Jones advises Subject the following:

Officer: "It is clear that you have information you are not sharing with me. We'll have to discuss your experiences before we can proceed."

Rapport Summary

In summary, rapport must be established to conduct a successful interview and successfully elicit information. Establishing rapport may not guarantee that you develop credible information but the absence of rapport will certainly impede your efforts. As demonstrated, rapport is established by showing patience and sincerity. Failure to employ these attributes will likely lead to failure. It is also important to know when rapport has been established to move ahead with the interview. Spending too much time establishing rapport by becoming too friendly and providing personal information about yourself can waste time and be unproductive.

Chapter 5 Elicitation

There are no fool-proof recipes for detecting deception and eliciting information, however, information is the best defense, as well as the most viable weapon in resolving any conflict, terrorism being no exception.

The journey we are about to take is designed to give law enforcement, intelligence officers, and others in need of collecting credible and reliable information, the tools necessary to improve their ability to gather valid and factual information.

The ultimate goal is to protect the American public against terrorists and the instruments of terror.

The focus here for the interviewer is to understand the difference between obtaining a confession and information collection. Understanding the difference requires a paradigm shift for some; the confession versus elicitation. Most of us are taught that confessions are motivated by fear and consequences and sometimes the use of hard techniques such as intimidation and threats may result in unreliable or fabricated confessions. Providing the Subject with justification for his/her guilty wrong-doing is the key to getting a confession.

The paradigm shift involves motivating the Subject to provide information by developing a relationship or bond with the interviewer. The use of "soft" techniques often yields more information. Information is developed using the Subject's emotions, values, and self-perceptions as motivators to provide information pertaining to the issue in question.

Elicitation is an art form intended to subtly extract information from a person in a fashion that closely resembles a social conversation.

Officer: Below, the officer begins the interviews by establishing rapport with the Subject. Simply explaining what is happening and what is expected can be enough to set the tone for questioning. The interviewer is in control.

Subject 5, I am Officer Jones, I have a few questions I need to ask you as part of our inspection process. Before we get started, is there something I can get for you.

Subject 5:
No, thank you.

Officer:
I need to ask you about your status in the United States. Can you …

Elicitation Summary

In summary, elicitation involves establishing a relationship with the Subject and using soft techniques. This combination is more likely to yield more information. Using the Subject's emotions, values, and self perceptions is the key to getting credible and reliable information.

Chapter 6 The Art of the Question

As mentioned in previous chapters, the primary goal of the interview is to elicit truthful and relevant information, not to obtain an admission of guilt. You should strive to get the suspect, witness, victim, or source talking, and keep him or her talking by using the appropriate questions.

We collect information in this fashion by subtly extracting it during what appears to be a casual conversation. The closer this activity appears to be conversational in nature, the better your chances of collecting information in a non-threatening fashion. This is the art of the question.

Understand in some situations, you may know the answers or think you have current information. Asking these questions can provide an opportunity to obtain updated information, establish a baseline by asking non-threatening type questions or identifying potential verbal/non-verbal responses. Every question should have a reason to be asked. When asking a person questions, keep the following types of information in mind to keep your line of questioning on target:

- Names, Address, Phone Numbers, and Relationships to:
  o Roommates, Friends, and Relatives
  o Points of Contacts
  o Business Associates

- Nationality and Place of Birth
- Injuries or Disabilities
- Recent Travels
- Finances
- Occupation, Training, Professional Associations, and Areas of Expertise (Especially With Possible WME/WMD Connections)

Is there hostile intent?

When embracing the role of "Intelligence/Informational collector," you will always find information can be useful and apply to anyone needing information from the boardroom to the border.

During the early stages of your "conversation" you should look to elicit biographic information about your Subject, to include their full legal name; other names they may have used; and their current address.

If the Subject is with a companion, has roommates or business associates, you should also elicit as much information as you can about these people. When doing this, look to determine the nature of the relationship your Subject has with the person in question.

If the Subject has special occupational or professional training, discuss his or her academic and professional credentials, particularly if the credentials are in a scientific arena with exposure to nuclear or biologic technology.

Remember, your goal is to elicit relevant information in a non-accusatory manner and to determine hostile intent.

Developing questions is an art form that requires patience, persistence, and flexibility. By carefully crafting the various types of questions you have at your disposal, you will be able to get even highly motivated person(s) intent on practicing deception to talk about areas of their concern. Once this happens, you can fine-tune discussions to harvest information you know is critical to the investigation at hand. As demonstrated in the following scenario:

> *Officer*:
> Where are you coming from today?
> *Subject 6*:
> Egypt.
> *Officer*:
> And where are you traveling to?
> *Subject 6*:
> Washington, DC
> *Officer*:
> And who are you visiting?
> *Subject 6*:
> Mr. Abdel Malak, who is my cousin.
>
> *The Officer does a data query on a computer.*
> *Under him is the caption:*

The query indicates that the address the passenger entered on his travel documents are listed to another gentleman Abdel Malak, who has a TIDE record for terrorist financing.

> *Officer*:
> Besides your cousin, who else at that address?

Effectively constructing and employing your questions when eliciting information is as important as having a good interview strategy. Knowing why we ask certain types of questions in a particular fashion is paramount as each question type has a particular purpose. Asking many questions of a Subject may seem tedious, but is required to fully understand the Who, What, When, Where, How, and Why's of the situation at hand. This is essential to gathering reliable and accurate information.

CLOSED-ENDED QUESTIONS

Close-ended questions are questions used to elicit a direct answer. Here are some ways that close-ended questions are used in an interview:

Officer:
The reason I stopped you today is part of the routine inspection process. Where are you coming from today?
Subject 7:
Egypt.
Officer:
And where are you traveling to?
Subject 7:
Washington, DC
Officer:
Are these all your bags?
Subject 7:
Yes.

OPEN-ENDED QUESTIONS

Open-ended questions are designed to elicit a narrative response to get the person talking and keep him talking. Open-ended questions should address a specific issue and not be overly broad or overreaching.

Here are some examples of open-ended questions:

Officer:
Could you tell me about your family?
Subject 8:
Yes, I am married and I have two sons and two daughters.
Officer:
Subject 8, we are investigating the attempted Sarin attack on a cruise ship. What knowledge do you have of this event?
Subject 8:
Officer, why would you say I was involved?

PRESUMPTIVE QUESTIONS

Presumptive questions are used to elicit information by including an unstated presumption into the question. A presumptive question must be based on two or more known facts from which a reasonable inference can be drawn. These types of questions allow the Subject to "acknowledge" or "confirm" information in a positive fashion that he believes you already know. This allows the Subject to save face and lets him know that you don't find what he's admitted to as being objectionable.

Here are some examples of presumptive questions and how they could be used:

62   *Barry McManus*

* What was your involvement in the cruise ship attack?
* Why did you and Ali stage the sarin gas attack on the cruise ship?
* What happened last night?

Scenario 9: Question Formulation

An Officer has stopped a vehicle that was spotted traveling at a high rate of speed. The officer requested Subject's drivers permit and vehicle registration. Upon requesting data checks on Subject's documents, subsequent query indicates that Abdel Malak lives at the address indicated on Subject's vehicle registration and that Malak has a TIDE (Terrorist Identities Data Mart Environment) record for terrorist financing. NCIC (National Crime Information Center) check also ascribes a "Detain and Question" indicator to Subject's record. Subject is transported to the station house where he is subsequently questioned.

Formulate a series of questions designed to elicit information about Subject 9's relationship with Malak.

Officer:
Subject 9, I'm Officer Jones. I'm sorry to have to detain you but you were driving recklessly and because of that, I have to ask you some questions. Is there anything I can get you before we start to talk?
Subject 9:
No Officer Jones, how can I help you? What did I do wrong?
Officer:
Your driver's license indicates that you live at 147 Laurel Ave. Is that your correct address?

Subject 9:
Yes Officer. I have lived there for about two years.

Officer:
Before coming to the Laurel Ave, where did you live?

Subject 9:
I am originally from Syria, but I came to the US about five years ago initially living in Florida. I came to the Laurel Ave address to take a job at the local airport.

Officer:
What do you do at the airport?

Subject 9:
I'm a bag handler with a local airline.

Officer:
That must be hard work with travel being as popular as it is here in the States. You must not have much time of your own.

Subject 9:
I work 12 hours a day officer, then I must go home and rest so that I can work the next day.

Officer:
You must have some form of relaxation to get your mind off of work. How do you spend your time when you're not working?

Subject 9:
I attend mosque in Northern Virginia and frequent activities sponsored by the mosque. This is the only time I get to see many of my friends and acquaintances.

Officer:
How often do you attend mosque?

Subject 9:
I attend the mosque every day just after work. I am usually there for the evening prayer after which I go home.

Officer:

Does your family join you at evening prayers?

***Subject* 9:**

I'm not married officer. Someday I hope to be but that day has not come.

***Officer*:**

This is an expensive area to live in for a young single person. Most people would have to have a roommate to help with the rent. Who are your roommates Subject 9?

***Subject* 9:**

I have only one roommate. He is Abdel Malak. I've known him since moving here.

***Officer*:**

How would you describe your relationship with Mr. Malak?

***Subject* 9:**

I would describe it as good. He occasionally goes to mosque with me and we'll often times eat together. I'd consider him to be a friend.

***Officer*:**

Tell me a little bit about Malak.

Exercise 1.

Identify each question listed below as close-ended, open-ended or presumptive.

1. **Officer:** Subject 9, I'm Officer Jones. I'm sorry to have to detain you but you were driving recklessly and because of that, I have to ask you some questions. Is there anything I can get you before we start to talk?
2. **Officer:** Your driver's license indicates that you live at 147 Laurel Ave. Is that your correct address?
3. **Officer:** Before coming to Main Street, where did you live?
4. **Officer:** What do you do at the airport?
5. **Officer:** That must be hard work with travel being as popular as it is here in the States. You must not have much time of your own.
6. **Officer:** You must have some form of relaxation to get your mind off of work. How do you spend your time when you're not working?
7. **Officer:** How often do you attend mosque?
8. **Officer:** Does your family join you at evening prayers?
9. **Officer:** This is an expensive area to live in for a young single person. Most people would have to have a roommate to help with the rent. Who are your roommates Subject 9?
10. **Officer:** How would you describe your relationship with Mr. Malak?
11. **Officer:** Tell me a little bit about Malak.

The correct answers are listed below.

- Closed-ended questions: e.g.1, 2, 3, 4, 5, 7 and 8
- Open-ended questions: e.g. 6, 10 and 11
- Presumptive questions: e.g. 9

Using the information, scenarios, examples, and exercises thus far, hopefully, you have been able to refine your interviewing techniques, sharpen your ability to pick out a lie and identify and understand the importance of history and culture and how it can impact your job when you engage someone from a different country with ideas, beliefs, norms and traditions different than your own.

To review, a closed-ended question is one used to elicit a direct answer. An open-ended question is a question designed to get the person talking. It generally calls for a narrative response. It should not be overly broad or overreaching; a presumptive question is one used to elicit information by adding a presumption (not stated in the interview) into the question. They are designed to lend the source or Subject to believe you have critical information that he or she is not aware of and allow him/her to "confirm" this information for you through the use of a presumptive question. Presumptive questions are generally based on two or more known facts from which you can draw a reasonable inference.

The following scenario(s) offers a window into interviewing individuals from a variety of backgrounds. It is not intended to be all inclusive. The best way to become effective at interviewing individuals from different backgrounds is to becoming a student of culture.

Scenario 10:
Background information:

Subject (a 37 year-old Pakistani male dressed in casual clothing) was stopped and questioned by train station security after he was acting suspiciously. When approached by the officers he appeared nervous and somewhat defensive as he spoke to the officers. While the Subject is carrying a US Passport, he claims to have been living in Pakistan for the past five years. He is now here to develop the textile/clothing business with several American retailers. He states that he has been working in the textile industry in Pakistan. Recently, the US has granted a higher import textile quota for Pakistan, he is here to exploit this policy and his knowledge of the "American system".

Subject describes himself as the vice president of international sales for the K Textiles Industries Ltd. This organization has various locations within Pakistan as well as in the Middle East where there is a high demand and market for the textile products. Subject admits to having traveled to the Middle East on several occasions regarding business related matters. There are no entries on his US passport indicating those visits.

The Subject explains that he also has a Pakistani passport as dual-citizenship is recognized between the two countries. He uses the Pakistani passport when he travels in the Middle East for safety reasons. As an American and a business executive, he would be a target for hostile individuals. He does not have his Pakistani passport with him. When questioned, the Subject states that he resides with a relative in the United States as he meets with his counterparts in the US.

Upon requesting data checks on Subject's documents and relatives, NCIC queries of Subject and his relative Daoud

SAEED a match was found with a NCIC warrant for narcotics and money–laundering. A query of SAEED residence indicated that someone by the name of Susan MATHEWS resided at the address and has a TIDE record with no date of birth or other biographical information. The TIDE was for possible association with terrorist financing. There is no other derogatory information. NCIC also ascribes a "Detain and Question" indicator to SAEED and MATHEW's record.

Subject explains that he lived in the United States for fifteen years before moving to Pakistan. He attended G M University in Virginia where he earned his MBA. He moved back to Pakistan after he was made a handsome offer. He hopes to use his skills to establish business relationship with US companies.

Select three possible commonalities that you could use to establish your rapport/conversations with the Subject.

1. Subject's education
2. Subject's religion
3. Subject's employment
4. Subject's family
5. Subject's accomplishments
6. Subject's political affiliations

Exercise 2.

Using the background information in the above scenario and applying what you have learned thus far, identify three possible commonalities that you would use to establish rapport.

Officer:
Subject 10:

I am Officer Jones. I'm sorry to have to detain you but because of your suspicious behavior and the call for assistance from the station security office we need to collect some additional biographical information.

Subject 10:

What suspicious behavior? I am just a little upset with my cousin and maybe I voiced my anger a little too loudly, but I don't think that's a crime Officer.

Officer:

I understand Subject 10, but could you help us help you and gather a little additional information about you sir?

Subject 10:

What do you need to know about me Officer?

Officer:

Well, could you tell me who this cousin is that you are trying to locate and has upset you so much.

Subject 10:

Well, my cousin's name is Abdel Malak and he lives at 147 Laurel Ave.

Officer:

Well, Subject 10, thank you for your cooperation. We apologize for the delays, but our information shows that an individual by the name David SAEED at the address 147 Laurel Ave. Our information also lists a Ms. Susan SMITH at the same address. Could you tell who is Ms. SMITH and the connection between the two, or did we copy the incorrect spelling of your cousin's name or address?

Subject 10:

Well officer, my cousin also uses the first James since he

arrived in the United States. So, the name is correct David SAEED and his address is 147 Laurel Ave.

Officer:

Well, what is the relationship between Mr. SAEED and Ms. SMITH?

Subject 10:

Well officer, David is my mother's sister son, and he should be like a brother to me but instead he very distant did not even offer to pick me up from the train station after all we have done for him. Susan SMITH is my wife. She is American and has chosen to use her maiden name instead of my name, Khan!

Officer:

Thank you Subject 10, you must understand that sometimes things can be confusing and incorrect information is collected and mistakes are made. Are there any concerns you have that you need to tell us about pertaining to your cousin or your wife?

Exercise 2 Solutions:

In Subject's culture, it would be easier and non-threatening to start a conversation with Subject 10 about his successes in business, and his educational accomplishments. These areas of discussion are generally less threatening and would allow just about anyone the opportunity to look for commonalities that would help the Subject to drop his defenses and barriers that people tend to show when they are concealing information for a various reasons.

The correct answers are 1, 3, and 5.

Helpful tip: In the Subject's culture, it would be impolite to address Subject's religion since it was not a point of discussion during the interview. Second, in Subject's culture it would not be considered polite to question someone directly about his immediate family. And, if there are two things to avoid in any interview environment it would be politics and religion unless the Subject chooses to address these topics. But remember, these two topics are so controversial the potential of losing rapport is sometimes great.

Summary

In summary, the most important elements to remember about conducting an interview are that the Art of Elicitation is the subtle extraction of information during a conversation, and the Art of the Question requires patience and flexibility. The key to the highly motivated true believer is to get him or her to talk about anything at first before we fine tune our discussions to get those answers we know are critical.

We collect information in this fashion by subtly extracting it during what appears to be a casual conversation. The closer this activity appears to be conversational in nature, the better your chances of collecting information in a non-threatening fashion. This is the art of elicitation.

"You go into the theater of the mind, build your own set and play out the drama. Perhaps there won't be applause, but your audience, namely yourself, is rapt with the show, believing it 100 percent."

– Anonymous

Chapter 7 The Use of Rapport-Based Elicitation
Themes and Stories

A theme or story is a rationalization or strategy to convince a person to provide you with relevant information that may not necessarily be to his advantage. As illustrated below, a theme or story will general:

- Suggest a justification or motive for the Subject's actions.
- Communicate that the interviewer understands why the Subject would take such actions.
- Allow the Subject to "save face" and provide information.

Foundation of a Theme or Story

When offering a theme, you should:
- Sound sincere, sympathetic, and understanding.
- Maintain trust and rapport.
- Use information and observations collected during interview.
- Include information that is relevant and believable.
- Continue listening.
- Repeat the theme if appropriate.

Stating an Elicitation Theme or Story

When stating a theme you may:

- Rationalize the action. *"You were just trying to make the world a better place and now realize . . . ."*
- Minimize the action. *"You never intended to harm innocent women and children."*
- Project the blame. *"This isn't your idea, it's just part of the struggle."*
- Use third-person language. *"Others have told me they've became disillusioned with the cause because of the harm it caused their families."*
- Focus on telling the truth vs. the action itself. *"What you've done in the past isn't a concern, we're just interested in getting to the correct information now."*

Chapter 8 Identifying and Overcoming Countermeasures

There are many thoughts on countermeasures as it relates to interrogation or eliciting information. Can countermeasures be effectively used to defeat your efforts to elicit information? If you think you are beaten then you are. But in reality, there's no definitive answer to this question. The best way to handle this issue is be prepared, know your Subject, and believe that everyone given the opportunity and good reason will lie to you. This requires you to practice, understand human behavior and be aware of cultural sensitivities. These efforts will increase your ability to elicit information. When you are confident in eliciting information and well-prepared, it will decrease your Subject's confidence and lessen the chance your efforts will be defeated by countermeasures. What is a countermeasure? Countermeasures can be defined as efforts (physical, psychological) that your Subject can use to prevent you from staying on target, designed to mislead you to make you believe they are telling you the truth and not hiding information. These tactics counter your efforts when successfully employed.

There are numerous books and web-pages available and accessible to anyone who searches that are designed to teach or train people how to defeat interviews and interrogations. It is the person eliciting information who is targeted by the Subject. The

Subject accesses the Interviewer the same way the Interviewer accesses the Subject. Subject's size up the interviewer and if they can manipulate them they will. As you read further in Chapter 10 on "Deceivers and Deceived", you will gain a full appreciation of those who deliberately deceived and the tactics they employed.

Common interviewer mistakes that make the Interviewer susceptible to countermeasures:

• Becoming angry and losing self-control.

Subject's gain the upper hand and often will bait the Interviewer to unnerve them to get them to lose control. Once done, the countermeasure is successful. The Interviewer loses the Subject. The Interviewer has allowed the Subject to bait him or her and the interview or elicitation is over.

Subjects may display arrogance by offending the Interviewer deliberately as a countermeasure.

If the Interviewer is unprepared, the Subject knows this and the Interviewer loses confidence while the Subject gains confidence knowing that the Interviewer does not have a clue and has missed important points or discrepancies provided by Subject during the interview. Another countermeasure a Subject may employ is getting the Interviewer to become too friendly. Interviewers need to remain on target and remember it is the Subject who should be providing the information and not the other way around.

Some other simple forms of behavioral countermeasures could be as simple as the following:

• Arriving late
• Wasting time during the interview

- Placing restrictions on the interview
- Leading the interview discussion into irrelevant areas
- Complaining
- Threatening political repercussion, legal actions, etc., against the Interviewer

Human beings draw close to one another by their common nature, but habits and customs keep them apart.

Confucian Proverb

Chapter 9 The Impact of Cultural Consideration

I have always believed that people are more alike than different, it's just those differences that we must understand.

Figure 1. Pakistani men on their way to work.

What is culture? "Culture is a set of learned beliefs, values and behaviors the way of life shared by the members of a society." (Society for Archaeology, 1996)

As an investigator, intelligence collector, police officer or business analyst, you must understand the cultures of the world. Whether it's the history and culture of Latin America, the Japanese concept of "I" based on Buddhism, Confucianism and Feudalism or the study of Islam, we must all take time to study.

Interview with a Middle Easterner

The Middle East is an area made up of 21 separate countries with vastly different countries with many cultures and many aspects touching their lives, religion being one. Like all true believers, Muslims feel their religion (Islam) and culture is better than anyone else's. So, when a Westerner asks a question, there may be confusion, such as when you ask:

Q: What about a sense of personal responsibility?

A: There is no sense of personal responsibility as we learn in American culture. That's why if you say to a Middle Easterner, "you lost it," he will say, "I didn't." partly to protect himself against accusation and partly if he lost it, it was meant to be lost, but he, personally, did not "cause" it to happen.

Q: What about something as simple as a handshake how would you greet a male Middle Easterner?

A: Generally, if you watch two Middle-Easterners meeting, they may shake hands – both hands go out to the other person. Then, both hands may move to the person's shoulders and there is a brief or enthusiastic hug, depending how well you know the other person. Then you may make the first move towards kissing the other person or you don't.

Q: Why shake both hands?

A: Always both hands because this shows your intentions are peaceful, that there's no dagger in the other hand.

Q: What about the strength of the handshake? In America a firm handshake shows strength of character.

A: I would say it depends. I would use less strength then normal in this country or else you may come across as hostile or crude.

Q: Are there something you can do to establish rapport between the American and Middle-East cultures?

A: It is always nice to mention some of the contributions towards Westerners culture by the Middle East. Such contributions would include astronomy as well as geometry. In addition, the Arabic numbering system, and the basic mathematics and sciences are used in technology.

"The key to the highly motivated true believer is to get him or her to talk about anything at first before we fine tune our discussions to get those answers we know are critical."

Source: The Violent True Believer: Functional Types, Needs/Sensitivities, and Interview Approaches, by Dr. J. Reid Meloy.

There are less effective and more effective ways of eliciting information from the highly motivated true believers. These individuals are motivated by deeply held beliefs serving as an agent of his or her god. They also may attempt to demean the interviewer as an "unbeliever" in silence. They draw their sustenance from internal beliefs and images. They typically do not consciously need the external sources of gratification (money, power, or sex). They also generally practice self-discipline and may not necessarily exhibit many emotions during an interview.

What is known is that the unwavering true believer well respond best if the Interviewer shows genuine interest sincerity.

Interview with a Latin American

Latin America is an area made up of 24 separate countries with different cultures. The cultural differences between Ecuador and Argentina alone are as diverse as those between France and China, and these ethnic and social differences make it very difficult to generalize about the area. Nevertheless, along with the variety in Latin American culture there are also similarities. Although, there are no steadfast rules, there are some general guidelines for understanding Latin American culture that may be helpful in establishing rapport.

Hospitality is one of the cornerstones of Latin culture. The minimum Latin American courtesy is to say "Hello," to shake hands, and to ask about one's family. Anything less is an insult and provokes a deep emotional reaction; it is difficult to communicate effectively with clenched teeth.

Figure 2. The author in Ecuador at the equator.

Figure 3. – Top photo: The author with a Colorado Indian outside in a village outside of Quito, Ecuador. Bottom photo: Colorado Indian, Quito, Ecuador

Figure 4. A pack mule outside La Paz, Bolivia

Figure 5. M-19, terrorist symbol on a street pole
in Bogota, Columbia.

With regards to body language, most North Americans stand
at "arm's length" when talking face-to-face while the Latin
American stands much closer. It is a common Latin complaint

that North Americans are cold, they keep you at arm's length and don't want to get close.

As similar to the Arab and Middle Eastern culture, Latin Americans of the same sex touch more than Americans of the same sex do. Young women will hold hands while walking. Men hug in greeting, while women commonly greet another woman with a light kiss on the cheek and always a handshake.

In the Latin American culture, handshaking is softer than in the United States. The firm, "frank," handshake is a hostile greeting in Latin America, while a soft handshake misleads Americans into thinking the person is a little less than honest and sincere.

Voice inflection, gestures, and emotion are important in any discussion for the Latin American, while we tend to consider softer tones, fewer tones, and fewer gestures and less emotion as the sign of a poised individual. The expressiveness and emotion in talking is again tied to the Latin concept on individuality and "Machismo".

The concept of "machismo" is widely known in the United States, but little understood. Usually North Americans connect it to sex alone. In Latin America, it is more the "essence of being masculine." The basic male outlook is involved, whether the man is tall, short, skinny, ugly or handsome. A "Macho" is confident! He is considered a good talker, to be both eloquent and witty.

**Figure 6. The author 10,000 feet above sea level
in La Paz, Bolivia**

As for eye contact, there is no general rule, though some Latin Americans are taught it is respectful to look down, to lower their eyes, when with someone in authority. To most westerners, this may look "shifty" but most don't realize a cultural pattern of respect is operating.

In the end, the Latin American like the Arab and Middle Eastern cultures are still in transition and largely traditional cultures, were personal relationships are the key to all functions. The "survival network" is still strong. People take priority over institutions and paper laws and regulations. The only way in general to get things moving is through a "friend" or a "friend of a friend."

Interview with an African

How do you tell a Sudanese from a Chadian, a Ethiopian from a Somalian? It may come as a surprise for many Africans to discover, but to most westerners, all Africans generally look the same to most non-Africans.

At the last count, there were 46 different countries, thus you get Southern Africans, East Africans, Central Africans, West Africans, and of course the Horn which is neither east, nor west, nor south, nor north. If you talk to most Africans, they claim they can tell an East African from a West African simply by looking at the person and a West African will tell you that they can tell a Gambian from a Sierra Leonean, and a Ghanaian from a Nigerian hundreds of miles away.

Figure 7. A fishing market in Dar Es Salaam, Tanzania.

As a westerner, it is very important to become knowledgeable of Africa's long cultural heritage. It is also important to become especially knowledgeable about the tremendous impact of the slave trade on Africa and the African's great sensitivity toward this subject.

Recognize that much of the African's sometimes "brashness" and outspoken materialism stems from most African countries' recent independence and nationalistic "growing pains."

As with the Arab, Middle Eastern and Latin American cultures, family and tribal ties are important. Become aware of how many different religions and traditional beliefs are intertwined for the African, guiding him in different directions under crisis conditions.

Interview with an Asian

The land boundary between Europe and Asia has never been officially designated. There are many different viewpoints concerning the border, which creates inconsistencies in a complete country count. The most common way to divide up and identify all Asian countries is listed below:

East Asia: China, Hong Kong S.A.R., Japan, Mongolia, North Korea, South Korea, Taiwan

South Asia: Bangladesh, Bhutan, India, Maldives, Nepal, Pakistan, Sri Lanka

Figure 10. Two Pakistani men on the streets in Karachi, Pakistan

Barry McManus

Figure 11. A mode of transportation in Pakistan

Figure 12. Boat in Kashmir, Pakistan.

Figure 13. Boat stopping at the "Cheap John" store
in Kashmir.

Central Asia: Afghanistan, Iran, Kazakhstan, Kyrgyzstan,
Tajikistan, Turkmenistan, Uzbekistan

Figure 14. The author and a friend in Afghanistan.

Southeast Asia: Brunei, Cambodia, East Timor, Indonesia, Laos, Malaysia, Myanmar, Philippines, Singapore, Thailand, Vietnam

Australia: Australia, New Zealand, **Pacific Island Countries, Papua New Guinea

The Pacific Island Countries include:

American Samoa, Cook Islands, Federated States of Micronesia, Federated States of Midway Islands, Fiji, French Polynesia, Guam, Kiribati, Marshall Islands, Nauru, New

Caledonia, Northern Mariana Islands, Palau, Pitcairn Islands, Solomon Islands, Tonga, Tuvalu, & Vanuatu. All total there are approximately 53 Asian countries. But remember, there are no definitive borders around Asia. With that in mind, let's generalize the culture of an Asian.

As in the many other cultures we have mentioned, the family relationship is strong and extends beyond the nuclear family. Greeting and partings should always include each person present and always begin with the eldest person present. As with other formal cultures, rapport being so important in meeting and understanding various cultures, avoid jumping into the subject matter immediately. Pleasantries and inquiries will open many doors down the road.

As in most formal reserve cultures in the Middle East and Asia, there is a general natural reserve and most are hesitant to open up with persons outside the family. Females are frequently accompanied by a male family member. The Asian is also known to talk around the subject matter and thus a direct approach may not work. In several instances, many younger people are taught not to have eye to eye contact with an older person when talking to them. This is not necessarily a form of evasion but a sign of respect.

Often the smile can be construed as agreement but in fact the smile is more of a covering of ones feeling. It does not indicate agreement.

In all cultures discussed, a quiet calm demeanor is the most effective attribute of establishing rapport and conversation. Raising your voice or showing anger lower your stature in their eyes.

In the end, to become a better collector of information, get to know other cultures.

"Who's going to believe a con artist?"
"Everyone, if he's good."

Chapter 10 The Deceivers and Deceived

Definition – A deceiver can be many things, a con artist, a liar, an individual who gains the trust of another only to benefit from that trust in some way. The deceived is the person on the receiving end of the game, the target, or the mark.

The ability to persuade others is not in itself abnormal. It is also not extraordinary to lie, misrepresent and to deceive. As far as special techniques for the identification and successful persuasion of victims, there is very little evidence in literature which suggests that deceivers have any special sensitivity or gifts of insights into the minds of others. The deceiver's confidence, freedom from remorse, lack of affection or empathy for others, the enjoyment of acting and theater and the use of hyperbole are all assets in operations. When a systematized approach is added to the skills of a deceiver, as for example, the understanding of the culture, beliefs and ideologies of a particular target he becomes prey to the skilled operative.

As for the victim (the deceived), the literature provides us very few clues as to what influences the deceived to develop trust to what the deceiver is saying or what he or she is doing.

Deceiving and being deceived has existed since the beginning of time. Con men, flim-flam man throughout the years have discovered various methods and schemes to beat gullible people out of their hard earned money. Today, con men or confidence men have changed or expanded from the simple confidence game to a riskier and complex business. Today, confidence men and women use their skills to deceive law enforcement, board room executives and intelligence officers in ways that could have serious implications to national security. Take as an example the 9-11 hijackers. These individuals could be categorized as con men. They use their street smarts, savvy and understanding of culture to get into the minds of the American people or other nations to impose harm to include using confidence games to obtain financing for their schemes of destruction.

Let's look closer at con men and women to understand how they are able to entrench themselves in a culture and society to con those around them, their target or mark. Con men are deceivers and their mark or target is the deceived. Those who seek to catch deceivers must become deceivers as well. This is similar to the investigator or detective putting themselves into the shoes of the criminal, or getting into the criminals mind. The same applies to trained deceivers. They must understand the mind of the con man or woman (the deceiver) to succeed at finding them out and stopping them from harming their victims.

As we consider the two, the deceiver and the deceived and the "War on Terror", the deceiver is clever and seeks a method to gain something of value to meet an end. The deceived is the mark or target. Someone considered to be gullible, trusting, an easy mark. The mark or gullible target usually has a weakness that has been identified by the deceiver. The Deceiver will find ways to gain the deceived's trust. Once they have hooked the person they manipulate that trust to their advantage.

These terms, which use confidence in the sense of "trust," date from the mid-1800s. They also gave rise to confidence man being known as the swindler.

The elements of the crime of the confidence game are (1) an intentional false representation to the victim as to some past or present fact . . . (2) knowing it to be false . . . (3) with the intent that the victim rely on the representation . . . (4) The representation being made to obtain the victim's confidence. . . and thereafter his money and property.

The grade of one's "intelligence" is totally unrelated to one's grade of vulnerability to getting deceived by experienced con men. Confidence tricks exploit human weaknesses like greed, dishonesty, vanity, but also virtues like honesty, compassion, or the "naïveté" of believing in the existence of something called "good faith". Just as there is no typical in depth profile for a swindler or a terrorist, neither is there one for their victims.

Footnotes

1 American Educational Research Association, American Psychological Association and the National Council on Measurement in Education (1999). *Standards for educational and psychological testing.* Washington, DC.

2 BBC News, (Jan. 2002). *A Brief History of Lying.* (p.2, 2-3). Retrieved Nov. 8, 2006 from http://news.bbc.co.uk/1/hi/uk/1740746.stm.

3 Ibid. (p.2, 4-5).

4 Ibid. (p.3, 4.)

5 Ibid. (p. 3 - 4, 7.)

6 Ibid.

7 Ibid.

8 Lykken, David Thoreson (1981). *A Tremor In the Blood: Uses and Abuses of The Lie Detector.* New York: McGraw-Hill Book Company, p. 26.

9 Segrave, Kerry (2004). *Lie Detectors: A Social History.* Jefferson, NC: McFarland & Company, Inc., Publishers, p. 12.

10 Carliste, Rodney, (Ed.). (2004). Scientific *American: Inventions and Discoveries.* New York: John Wiley and Sons, Inc., p. 359.

11 Matte, James Allan (1996). *Forensic Psychophysiology Using the Polygraph: Scientific Truth Verification – Lie Detection.* Williamsville, NY: J.A.M. Publications, p. 20.

12 Marston, William Moulton (1938). *The Lie Detector Test.* New York: Richard R. Smith, p. 51.

13 Singel, Kati. (2005). "The Origin of the Modern Polygraph." In *The Polygraph: The Modern Lie Detector* (p. 3). Retrieved March 3, 2006, from http://www.umw.edu/hisa/resources/Student%20Projects/Sing el/students/students.umw.edu/_ksing

14 Larson, John A. (1969). *Lying and Its Detection: A Study of Deception and Deception Tests.* Montclair, NJ: Patterson Smith, pp. 257-285.

15 Matte, James Allan (1996). *Forensic Psychophysiology Using the Polygraph: Scientific Truth Verification – Lie Detection.* Williamsville, NY: J.A.M. Publications, p. 20.

16 Ibid.

17 Ibid.

18 Stoelting Co. – The Analog Polygraph (2006). Retrieved March 3, 2006 from http://www.stoeltingco.com/polygraph/store/viewlevel3.asp?k eyword1=29&keyword3=83

19 Stoelting Co. – The Analog Polygraph (2006). Retrieved March 3, 2006 from http://www.stoeltingco.com/polygraph/store/viewlevel3.asp? keyword1=29& keyword3=83

20 Segrave, Kerry (2004). *Lie Detectors: A Social History.* Jefferson, NC: McFarland & Company, Inc., Publishers, p. 12.

21 TVSA3: Voice Stress Analysis Freeware (1999). *About Voice Stress Analysis.* (p. 2, Really! Try to get it! ¶ 2) Retrieved March 3, 2006 from http://www.whatreallyhappened.com/RANCHO/POLITICS /VSA/truthvsa.html.

22 Ibid.

23 Brown, Troy E., Ph.D.; Ryan, Andrew H., Jr., Ph.D.; and Senter, Stuart M., Ph.D. (2003). *Ability of the Vericator™ to Detect Smugglers at a Mock Security Checkpoint* (Department of Defense Polygraph Institute Report No. A019114). Abstract retrieved March 10, 2006, from http://www.stormingmedia.us/01/0191/A019114.html.

24 Ibid.

25 Cohen, Hal. (2002). "Polygraphs could be history, honest: thermal imaging may help flush out the liars" in *The Scientist*, p.8 as cited in "Lie Detection: The Science and Development of the Polygraph." (*illumin. . . A Review of Engineering in Everyday Life*; Issue ii: Volume 6) To, Katherine. Retrieved March 10, 2006 from

http://illumin.usc.edu/article.print.php?articleID=78

26 Holden, Constance. (2001). "Panel Seeks Truth in Lie Detector Debate" in *Science,* p. 967 as cited in "Lie Detection: The Science and Development of the Polygraph." (*illumin . . . A Review of Engineering in Everyday Life*; Issue ii: Volume 6) To, Katherine. Retrieved March 10, 2006 from http://illumin.usc.edu/article.print.php?articleID=78

27 Carroll, Jon. (1997). "Digital Polygraph Uses a Special Keyboard to Determine When the Person Using It Is Lying" in *Computer Life*, p. 150 as cited in "Lie Detection: The Science and Development of the Polygraph." (*illumin, A Review of Engineering in Everyday Life*. Issue ii: Volume 6) To, Katherine. Retrieved March 12, 2006 from http://illumin.usc.edu/article.print.php?articleID=78

28 Ibid.

29 Perina, Kaja. (2002). "Brain Scans May Be Foolproof Lie Detectors" in *Psychology Today,* p. 11 as cited in "Lie Detection: The Science and Development of the Polygraph." (*illumin, A Review of Engineering in Everyday Life*. Issue ii: Volume 6) To, Katherine. Retrieved March 12, 2006 from http://illumin.usc.edu/article.print.php?articleID=78

30 Ibid.

31 Slotnick, Rebecca Sloan. (2002). "Diogenes: New Lamp" in *American Scientist,* p. 127-8 as cited in "Lie Detection: The Science and Development of the Polygraph." (illumin, A

Review of Engineering in Everyday Life. Issue ii: Volume 6) To, Katherine. Retrieved March 13, 2006 from http://illumin.usc.edu/article.print.php?articleID=78

32 Bean, Matt. (2001, December 17). "Special Report – The Science of Lies: From the Polygraph to Brain Finger-printing and Beyond" in *CourtTV.com-TOP NEWS*. Retrieved March 13, 2006 from http://www.courttv.com/news/feature/liedetection_ctv.html

33 Ibid.

34 Ibid.

APPENDIX A:

Glossary

al-Qaeda – translation: (*The Base*) a Radical Islamic organization founded in Afghanistan. Led by Osama bin Laden.

Buddhism – Buddhism is considered the fifth-largest religion in the world behind Christianity, Islam, Hinduism, and traditional Chinese religion.

Cachet – a seal affixed to a document.

CIA – Central Intelligence Agency.

Confucianism – is a Chinese ethical and philosophical system originally developed from the teachings of the early Chinese sage Confucius. Confucius was the founder of the teachings of Confucianism. Confucianism is a complex system of moral, social, political, philosophical, and religious thought which has had tremendous influence on the culture and history of East Asia up to the 21st century.

Coptic Christian – is the official name for the largest Christian church in Egypt.

Culture – Set of learned beliefs, values and behaviors the way of life shared by the members of a society.

Countermeasure – Efforts (physical, psychological) that your Subject can use to prevent you from staying on target, designed to mislead you to make you believe they are telling you the truth and not hiding information.

Cingulate cortex – is a part of the brain situated in the medial aspect of the cortex.

Deception Detection – activities of an individual that can be observed with the usual human senses without physical contact.

Feudalism – a general set of reciprocal legal and military obligations among the warrior nobility of Europe during the Middle Ages, revolving around the three key concepts of lords, vassals, and fiefs.

FBI – Federal Bureau of Investigation.

Lie – A false statement deliberately presented as being true; a falsehood. The American Heritage® Dictionary.

Terrorist – is one who engages in acts of murder, rape or other violent crime, usually against civilians, under the guise of political activism.

Quran – Islamic Holy Book, given by Allah to the Prophet Mohammad.

Middle East

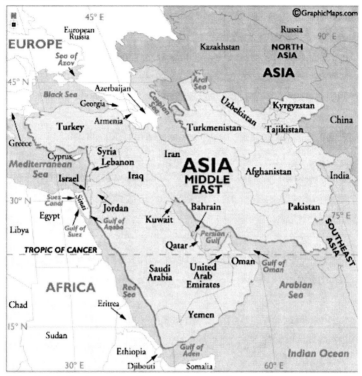

The Middle East (*or West Asia*) sits where Africa, Asia and Europe meet. The countries of the Middle East are all part of Asia, but for clarity reasons we geographically show them here as a separate landmass.

Opinions vary as to what countries make up *the modern definition* of the Middle East. Historically, Armenia and Azerbaijan have been long associated with the Middle East, but in recent years, some sources now consider them to be more closely aligned with Europe based on their modern economic and political trends. We have moved in that direction, and the same applies for the island country of Cyprus, as it does for Georgia, the former Russian republic.

The African country of Egypt is still thought (*by some*) to be in the Middle East, as well as the northern African countries that border the Mediterranean Sea.

We attempt here to show the *modern definition*, but in world of geography, there are often many answers or (*personal or political opinions*) to what appears to be a simple question.

Muslim – Followers of Islam are called Muslims.

Interrogation – An accusatory procedure designed to elicit from a subject/suspect, an acknowledgement that he or she did not tell the truth.

Islam – in Arabic means 'submission', or specifically, submission to the Allah's will and obedience to His law.

Elicitation – is the subtle extraction of information of information during a conversation.

Rapport – A feeling of harmonious connection between people or groups of people.

Theme – A justification or motive for the Subject's actions.

Polygraph –
(commonly referred to
as a *lie detector*) is an
instrument that
measures and records
several physiological
responses such as blood
pressure, pulse,
respiration and skin
conductivity while the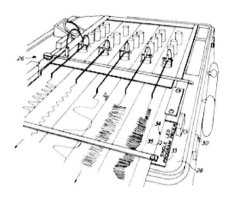
subject is asked and answers a series of questions. The polygraph
measures physiological changes caused by the Sympathetic Nervous
System during questioning. Within the Federal Government, a
polygraph examination is also referred to as a **psychophysiological
detection of deception** (PDD) examination.
Polygraph results are sometimes recorded on a chart recorder.

Voice Stress Analysis – is a newer technology than polygraph,
yet it is as controversial. VSA technology records psychophysiological stress responses that present in human voice, when a
person suffers psychological stress in response to a stimulus
(question) and where the consequences of lying may be dire for
the subject being 'tested'.

Facial thermal imaging – Thermal imaging facial recognition
systems are based on the principle that infrared cameras can
capture unique heat emission patterns from a person's face.

Iran Contra – (also **Iran gate**), was a political scandal
occurring in 1987 as a result of earlier events during the Reagan
administration in which members of the executive branch sold

weapons to Iran, an avowed enemy, and illegally used the profits to continue funding rebels, the Contras, in Nicaragua.

Hostile Intent – The threat of imminent use of force by a foreign force, terrorist(s), or organization against the United States.

Behavioral Analysis – the act of interpreting a person's behavior.

Brain Fingerprinting – records an electric signal called a MERMER emitted by the brain before the body physically reacts.

(MRI) – Magnetic resonance imaging.

Plethysmograph galvanic skin response – **Galvanic skin response**: A measure of physiological arousal determined by the amount of decrease in the skin's resistance to electricity purportedly due to an increase in sweat gland activity. **Plethysmograph:** A device used for finding variations in size of a segment of the body due to variations in the amount of blood passing through or contained in that segment.

USCBP – United States Custom and Border Protection.

Secondary Inspection – A separate, more thorough screening of some passengers at an airport or elsewhere. Passengers are selected for secondary inspection at random or because they have aroused suspicion by doing such things as purchasing a one-way ticket or paying in cash. Also called secondary screening.

Presumptive question – Question used to elicit information by including an unstated presumption into the question. A presumptive question must be based on two or more known facts from which a reasonable inference can be drawn.

Save face – Face is the desire to not appear weak or to look bad in the eyes of others.

True Believer – Term coined by Eric Hoffer, a person totally consumed by a cause. True believers act with similar behavioral characteristics no matter what cause they champion. They are willing to take extreme actions, including violence, to achieve the objectives of their cause, and they accept no criticism, dissent, or alternative philosophies. They believe that they cannot be wrong and that their philosophy explains all the realities of social life.

Protest – A statement made by the person practicing deception designed to continue the interviewer.

WorldCom – WorldCom has admitted orchestrating one of the largest accounting frauds in history.
Chief Executive Bernie Ebbers borrowed hundreds of millions from the firm to underwrite the inflated prices he had paid for the company's own shares.

Enron – When energy giant Enron reported its third quarter results last October, it revealed a large, mysterious black hole that sent its share price tumbling.
The company admitted that it had inflated its profits by $3.8bn (£2.5bn) between January 2001 and March 2002.
The firm was already shrouded in scandal after the departure of its founder Ebbers, in April.

The US financial regulator – the Securities Exchange Commission – launched an investigation into the firm and its results.

Enron then admitted it had inflated its profits, sending shares even lower.

Once it became clear that the firm's success was in effect an elaborate scam – a chorus of outraged investors, employees, pension holders and politicians wanted to know why Enron's failings were not spotted earlier.

The US government is now thought to be studying the best way of bringing criminal charges against the company.

Where it all began – Enron's HQ in Houston

Andersen – Attention quickly turned to Enron's auditors – Andersen.

The obvious question was why did the auditors – charged with verifying the true state of the company's books – not know what was going on?

Andersen reacted by destroying Enron documents, and on 15 June a guilty verdict was reached in an obstruction of justice case.

The verdict signaled an end to the already mortally wounded accountancy firm.

This wasn't the first time Andersen's practices had come under scrutiny – it had previously been fined by the SEC for auditing work for waste-disposal firm Waste Management in the mid-1990s.

The Andersen case raises a wider question about accounting in the US and how it might restore its reputation as the guarantor of the honest presentation of accounts.

Andersen's David Duncan faces the music

Adelphi – Telecoms company Adelphia Communications filed for bankruptcy on 25 June.

The sixth largest American cable television operator is facing regulatory and criminal investigations into its accounting.

The company has restated its profits for the past two years and admitted that it didn't have as many cable television subscribers as it claimed.

The firm has dismissed its accountants, Deloitte & Touché.

Xerox – In April, the SEC filed a civil suit against photocopy giant Xerox for misstating four years' worth of profits, resulting in an overstatement of close to $3bn.

Xerox negotiated a settlement with the SEC with regard to the suit.

As part of that agreement, Xerox agreed to pay a $10m fine and restate four years' worth of trading statements, while neither admitting, nor denying, any wrongdoing.

The penalty is the largest ever imposed by the SEC against a publicly traded firm in relation to accounting misdeeds.

Tyco – In early June, the US District Attorney extended a criminal investigation of the firm's former chief executive, Dennis Kozlowski.

Dennis Kozlowski – the man behind the creation of the Tyco conglomerate – is charged with avoiding $1m in New York state sales taxes on purchases of artwork worth $13m.

The SEC enquiry into Tyco is understood to relate solely to Mr. Kozlowski – but there are investor fears the probe could reveal accounting irregularities.

Last week, Tyco said it has filed a lawsuit against one of its former directors, Frank Walsh, for taking an unauthorized fee of $20m.

Global Crossing – Global Crossing was briefly one of the shiniest stars of the hi-tech firmament.

The telecoms network firm filed for Chapter 11 bankruptcy on 28 January.

The peculiar economics of bandwidth meant that firms could drum up the appearance of lively business by trading network access with each other.

They could effectively book revenues when in many cases no money at all changed hands.

US regulators are now looking closely at the collapse, questioning whether it is another case of a company flattering its figures.

Qwest – Qwest, the third-largest US regional phone company, became the target of both prosecutors and regulators in 2002, after it restated £2.2bn in revenues.

In April, Nacchio was found guilty of 19 counts of insider trading. He was acquitted on 23 counts.

Merrill Lynch – In this atmosphere of corporate distrust, the role of investment banks has also faced increased scrutiny.

Analysts were suspected of advising investors to buy stocks they secretly thought were worthless. The rationale for this 'false advice' was that they might then be able to secure investment banking business from the companies concerned.

Merrill Lynch reached a settlement with New York attorney general Eliot Spitzer. The settlement imposed a $100m fine upon Merrill but demanded no admission of guilt.

Under the deal, Merrill Lynch has agreed to sever all links between analysts' pay and investment banking revenues.

(CAM). – Cardio Activity Monitor.

Forensic Pychophysiologist. – Polygrapher.

(PSE). – Psychological Stress Evacuator.

(VSA). – Voice Stress Analyzer.

(CVSA). – Computerized Voice Stress Analyzer.

ACKNOWLEDGMENTS

To my family, especially my wife, who played an important role in encouraging me to share my philosophy of taking action as a key to success.

A special thanks to my agents Cynthia Lemay and Kat Quevedo who served as the avant-garde and the behind the scenes contributor for focus, direction, and patience to do this one "thing right the first time."

Thank you to those who have had a special impact on the development of this book existentially and analytically, Mr. Terry Wachtell and Mr. Tim James.

Particular thanks to those friends and colleagues who have encouraged me and provided insight into the murky waters of contracts and publishing, The Honorable Eugene Sullivan, Danielle Saunders and Brad Juneau.

I am particularly grateful to Hollis Helms, CEO of Abraxas Corporation, for his years of support academically during my times at Oxford, and for his overall unwavering faith in the many new ideas and endeavors that I have mustered over the past 4 ½ years.

Most importantly, and with a sense of pride, I dedicate this book to 1st Lieutenant Kurt Martine, a US Army National Guard who touched my life with his courage in the biggest battle of all, the fight for survival. We love you Kurt.

To all of you friends, family, and trusted colleagues, not mentioned by name, I will forever be grateful.

INDEX

The author in New Delhi, circa 1980's.

About the Author

Barry L. McManus, Vice President of Deception Detection Services of Abraxas Corporation in McLean, Virginia joined the Central Intelligence Agency in 1977 with a degree in Sociology as a staff security officer in the Office of Security, after serving five years on the Metropolitan Police Department in Washington, D.C. Mr. McManus served on the West Coast and on the DCI protective staff with the former Director of Central Intelligence Agency William Casey. On the Staff, Mr. McManus spent most of his time abroad before finding his home in the Polygraph Division in November 1982, where he served the remainder of his Agency career. He served in all Polygraph branches, worked as a line-supervisor domestically, and served as Office Chief of an overseas polygraph office.

Mr. McManus returned to the excitement of the technical side of polygraph after some years in management and became an expert examiner and interrogator. To reach "expert" level in the operational field, an examiner must be thoroughly knowledgeable of the overseas environment and demonstrate superior competence in polygraph techniques. Mr. McManus took language training and other necessary training required of an overseas operator. In this role, Mr. McManus was involved primarily in support of the Directorate of Operations. His primary mission was conducting high-gain, high-risk cases. Mr. McManus has taken his role very seriously. "When dealing with human lives, you have a major impact. You have to respect that responsibility."

Mr. McManus has extensive professional experience in the Middle East, Africa, Europe and Latin America. His Agency career has taken him to more than 130 countries. An Associate Professor in the Administration of Justice, Mr. McManus earned a B.A. in Sociology at Loyola College; an M.A. in Organizational and Security Management at Webster University; and is currently completing work on a Doctorate of Arts in Higher Education at George Mason University. Mr. McManus is noted for his contribution in supporting the fight against Terrorism. For his service to the national security of the United States, Mr. McManus received the CIA's Career Intelligence Medal.

Printed in the United States
208387BV00005B/19-30/P

9 780981 585505